COPYRIGHT NOTICE

For more information about *My TV/Radio Interview Tactics & Checklists*; individual orders; bundled orders, discounts for bulk-quantity purchases; audio products; interviews; information on seminars; JV opportunities; mentoring/consulting; booking the author to speak at your next seminar, workshop or event; please contact the author at any of his websites:

BARTSMITH.COM
TVGUEST.COM

INCOME DISCLAIMER: Every effort has been made to accurately represent the subject nature of this book and all its potential. Even though most industries are ones where a person can "write their own ticket" in terms of earning potential, there is "no guarantee" that you will earn any money using the teachings, lessons and ideas found in this book. Any examples provided are not to be interpreted as a promise or guarantee of earnings. Earning potential is entirely dependent upon the sincere effort and the effective use of what is found in this book and on your own individual effort, circumstances and more. That said, here's to your success.

TABLE OF CONTENTS

Whether you're after TV, radio, podcast, YouTube.com interviews or any other type of interview, this book is for you!

Read through it, digest what's in it, implement every applicable interview tactic, and execute every checklist item I discuss and I know your interviews will *EXPLODE* with outright enthusiasm and a hunger to do as many interviews as you can until you've reached your desired outcome, which is usually more exposure, more branding, more name recognition, more sales, ... you name it! At least, for me, that's why I enjoy interviewing. Plus, they're also ... *A LOT OF FUN!*

Message From The Author

PART 6

Here Are **10 Ways You Can** Personally **Improve** Your **Interview Skills** So You Come Across As A Seasoned **"Professional Interviewer"** Every Time!

PART 7

My Personal TV/Radio
Interview Checklist

THAT'S A WRAP

My TV/Radio Interview Tactics & Checklists
Summary & Words Of Encouragement

Bart's Other Books

TVGuest.com Directory

MESSAGE FROM THE AUTHOR

I'm really excited you picked up this book! Are you ready to tell the world what you do? Ready to be in the spotlight? ***"Today's guest is an expert in _____. Please help me welcome YOUR NAME to the show!"*** That has such a great ring to it, doesn't it? Well, get used to it. You're going to be hearing it a lot, and because you're going to be hearing that a lot and getting on a ton of shows, it's best you dive deep into this book before you do!

I've tried to tap as much of my own interview know-how and experience into this one book so your interviews R.O.C.K. I share tips that have worked consistently for me and perhaps they will help you with your interviews, personal or business. I'm confident that these tried and true checklists and tactics will get you, too, in front of the right people.

In advance, here's to your first (or next) interview after having read through this book. I can't wait to hear about your reaction when a host says to you, ***"GREAT SHOW! Great interview. You're really good. I should have you back again!"*** Yeah, that's a good way to kick this book off, isn't it? C'mon, let's get started!

Bart Smith

BART SMITH
BartSmith.com
TVGuest.com
ReallyFastBooks.com
BartsCookies.com

PART 1

Are You **Getting Interviewed?** Yes, Great! No, Why Not? Are Your **Interviews Effective**? Are You **Getting Interviewed Enough**?

TVGuest.com

GREAT QUESTIONS, EH? Let me ask you a few more:

- Are you getting interviewed **soon**?

- Have you been interviewed **lately**?

- When was the **last time** you were interviewed?

- What was the **largest audience of listeners,** subscribers or viewers you ever interviewed in front of and **how long ago** was that interview?

- What was the **greatest thing that resulted** from you being interviewed (i.e., a ton of sales/calls for your help, more interview invitations, etc.)?

- **Have you ever** been interviewed? Do you want to be interviewed?

Good questions, eh? How'd you do? Being interviewed is typically something most people don't do on an everyday basis. Although, if you know that interviews can help you reach your target audience, you could or should be doing them every day or at least 1-3 times per week.

Why are interviews an important part of your marketing plan?

For these very reasons:

- **Interviews are FREE to you,** for the most part. Sure, you could pay a publicity firm a couple thousand dollars to get you on some big TV/radio stations, and that investment could yield a nice return based on how far and wide you're seen and what you're getting interviewed about.

- **Interviews get you in front of your target market**, which is a good thing, especially if that audience is in the 1,000's multiplied by per week/month.

- Interviews can **generate sales** and cause your **phone to ring** and your **website to experience a flood of traffic!**

- Interviews with you that get archived on a show's website are **great for SEO** (Search Engine Optimization) and **"link juice"** when they **link back to your website**. *(Definition: Link juice is a term used in the SEO world to refer to the value or equity passed from one page or site to another. This value is passed through hyperlinks. Search engines see links as votes by other websites that your page is valuable and worth promoting. When you get interviewed multiple times per month, eventually, you'll have a number of websites linking back to you. THIS IS GOOD FOR SEO!)*

- Interviews **work better than ads** because you're in front of people for 15-45 minutes (or more), unlike ads for only a few seconds. There's a time and a place for ads, yes, but the power of interviewing is awesome.

So, as you can see, there are plenty of solid reasons why you should pursue getting interviewed as soon as you're ready to be interviewed.

How do get interviewed?

There are a few ways to get interviewed, many of which, are easy to go after, obtain and secure. Here's how I often go about it. First, I go hunting for shows that complement what it is I want to get interviewed about and where the target audience will be ultra receptive to what I have to share with them.

- **Find shows you like listening to or watching and find a way to get interviewed by the host.** Often times, these shows have a website that gives the opportunity for people like you and me to submit a request to be guests on their shows. Look for it or just go directly to their contact page and say the same thing. "Hi, I really like your show. I'm an author and would like to be a guest on your show to talk about ___ (topic). You can find out more about me on my INTERVIEW ME page at my website. Just go to YourSite.com/interviewme ... I look forward to hearing from you. ~ Your Name"

- Go to websites like **BlogTalkRadio.com, LATalkRadio.com, Apple iTunes Podcasting, Live365.com, Speaker.com, PodcastPeople.com, PodBean.com, ShoutCast.com and RadioGuestList.com**, for example. Get on their lists so they can send you interview requests weekly. Look up similar sites using search queries like, "get interviewed, be a guest on our show" or "authors wanted guest interviews" or "be a guest on our show." Spend time sifting through these websites to learn how to get on their show.

- **Pay to get a publicity firm to place you on high-level TV and radio shows.** Fees range between $500 to $5,000 per interview or a bundle of interviews. Is it worth it? YES! BUT, get interviewed 10-30 times first on the smaller stations just to get your talking points down and learn what interviewers respond to, soundbites that audiences and hosts want to hear you say, etc.

Where and how can you (learn) to get ready to be interviewed?

By reading this book, for starters, of course. That's why I wrote it! Seriously, when you go through these special reports and sections within these pages, I just know you'll be fast on your way to chasing after tons of interviews, getting interviewed and reaping the benefits of getting interviewed with class and confidence.

Learn To Write A Book At BartSmith.com/training & Start Interviewing

WHERE ARE YOUR ...

Video Interviews

TO HELP YOU GET MORE INTERVIEWS???

☑ **SHOW HOSTS** What You're Like **ON CAMERA** ...

☑ **PRACTICE & REHEARSE** Being Interviewed **ON CAMERA** ...

☑ **GET MORE INTERVIEWS** Because You Look/Sound **GREAT ON CAMERA** ...

Learn How To Get "Author Interviews" & Prepare For Them

interview questions

fulfillment ready

website done

well rehearsed

free offer ready

talking points ready

upsell pitch

10 Great Ways To Improve Your

INTERVIEW SKILLS

So You Come Across As A Seasoned Professional Interviewer Every Time!

Get A Profile Listing On TVGuest.com & Get More Interviews

Lastly, we have the ultimate in INTERVIEW CHECKLISTS. This happens to be one of my favorites of the 70+ business and marketing checklists I developed in **My Checklists** book. I can't wait for you to **check** it out.

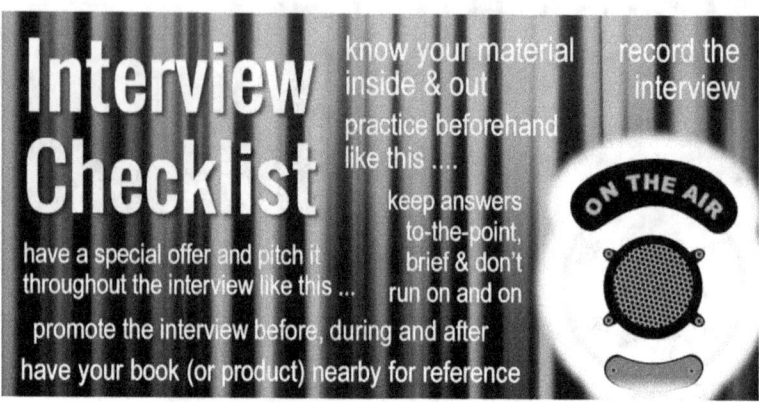

So, as you can see, you've got a lot waiting for you in the area of "interview training" moving forward. Can you just imagine how more improved your interview game will become once you read and take advantage of what you will learn in this book? You bet! Hey, let's get to the next part in this series. You're doing great!

PART 2

Where Is Your "Interview Me" Web Page On Your Website?

TVGuest.com

WHAT IS THE PURPOSE OF AN "INTERVIEW ME" WEB PAGE?

Basically, an "Interview Me" web page is designed to:

1. **HELP you get interviewed faster.** By having this page ready to go, you can easily reach out to dozens of shows to interview you knowing their host/producer will be pleased to know you're organized, prepared and available to go at a moment's notice.

2. **HELP those who want to interview you do their job faster/easier.** Having an "Interview Me" page on your website with all the right sections, content and information will help hosts prepare for your upcoming interview.

The "Interview Me" web page was something I came up with a long time ago to help TV, radio and podcast show hosts who asked to interview me. In this way, they can quickly and conveniently gather the information they require to do just that.

WHAT DOES AN "INTERVIEW ME" WEB PAGE LOOK LIKE?

Basically, an "Interview Me" web page is easy to create, whether your website is built with Systeme.io, Groove Pages, WordPress, Wix, SquareSpace, etc. It's designed specifically to provide key information about you and your topic for show interview decision makers, hosts and producers to get what they need regarding your interview, print it for their convenience and prepare for the interview.

Having a page like this makes it super easy to go after interviews, because all you really need to do is contact them, tell them to check out your *"Interview Me"* web page and let them get back to you. This is what it looks like:

TITLE OF YOUR BOOK
Subtitle Of Your Book

THIS BOOK IS ABOUT autem veleum de iriure dolor in hendrerite in vulputate velitobe esset molestie, vel illum et iusto odio dignissims quita blandit zzril delenit augue duis dolore tev feugait nulla facilisi.

AUTHOR BIO

AUTHOR'S NAME has been ipsum dolor sit amet, consectetuer adipiscing elit, sed diam nonummy euismod tincidunt ut laoreet dolore magna aliquam erat sed diam volutpat.

INTERVIEW QUESTIONS

1. Lorem ipsum dolor sit amet nonummy?
2. Lorem ipsum dolor sit amet nonummy?
3. Lorem ipsum dolor sit amet nonummy?
4. Lorem ipsum dolor sit amet nonummy?
5. Lorem ipsum dolor sit amet nonummy?
6. Lorem ipsum dolor sit amet nonummy?

CONTACT INFO

You can reach AUTHOR'S NAME and get his book in print, audio and eBook format at:

www.YourWebsite.com

SCHEDULE AN INTERVIEW

Click this link to schedule an interview with AUTHOR'S NAME or call 000-000-0000 to book a time/date over the phone.

HEAR SAMPLE INTERVIEWS

Click this link to hear samples of past interviews with AUTHOR'S NAME to give you an idea of what your interview could be like. Get ready for an amazing interview!

PREVIEW THE BOOK

Click this link to read and hear sample excerpts from **TITLE OF BOOK**.

PRINT THIS PAGE

Click this link to print a **Word .doc** version of this page for your use in taking notes, modifying questions and printing it for your convenience before / during the interview.

IMAGES FOR YOUR USE

Feel free to right-click, save and use the following large images for your needs.

You can see a number of live examples at any of my websites, such as:

BartSmith.com/interviews

WHATS GOES ON A TYPICAL "INTERVIEW ME" PAGE

As you can see from the illustration on the previous page, you have these key areas to fill in with content, information, images, etc.

1. **Interview Topic Title**

2. **Interview Topic Introduction** (1-3 paragraphs)

3. **Your Biography** (1-2 paragraphs)

4. **Interview Questions** (5-10)

5. **How To Contact You** (Call, eMail, etc.)

6. **How To Schedule An Interview** (Call, eMail, etc.)

7. **Sample Interviews** (Audio or video format.)

8. **Preview This** _____ (i.e., Book, Product, Service, etc.)

9. **Print This Page** (Easy to find button/downloadable link to the PDF version of the "Interview Me" page.)

10. **Images** For Their Use (i.e., Head shot, full-body shot, front book cover image, product image, etc.)

If you can think of other sections related to your particular interview topic, go ahead and add them. Again, these are just the essentials.

HOW DO YOU GET AN "INTERVIEW ME" WEB PAGE?

Basically, you build it like any other web page on your website. Again, look at the *"Interview Me"* page examples on my websites to get an idea of how they're designed. Then, ask your webmaster to build this page for you after you've accumulated all the necessary information needed for it.

Also, build one of these pages for each book you write or topic you want to get interviewed about. Once you have these in place, you'll be even more confident to reach out to show hosts to ask them to interview you. I know, because I've followed this formula for years and it works like a charm.

PART 3

Where Is Your
"Media Room"
Web Page On
Your Website?

TVGuest.com

Home   Get The Book   Get The Audio   Take The

Press Room & Media Inforn

Thank you, for your interest in **Laws Of The Bedroom**™
author of *Laws Of The Bedroom*™, Bart Smith, and what h
come back often to see what's new!

- ✹ Media Contact Information
- ✹ Interview Bart Smith, The Author
- ✹ Radio Interviews (Previously Recorded)
- ✹ Interview Questions
- ✹ Podcasting Shows
- ✹ Speaking Topics & Presentations
- ✹ Photo Image Gallery
- ✹ Biography Information
- ✹ About Laws Of The Bedroom
- ✹ Rave Reviews about "The Laws"

These pages are updated frequently, so please check back

What is a Media Room?

A Media Room (also called a press room) is a section on your website that provides members of the news media or anyone else interested in interviewing you with information about you, your book/product/company, photographs, press releases, interview questions, your press kit, and other vital necessities to help them "do their job!"

Why do you need a Media Room?

Getting free publicity and using the media to get the word out about what it is you do is one of the most under used methods of marketing you could spend time doing.

Remember this quote when dealing with the media ... "Help them do their job!" When I first heard that expression, I never forgot it, and neither should you. What does it mean? "Help them to do their job?" It means, don't make members of the media and other people struggle trying to get information about you so they can conduct that interview with you or write about you for their paper.

The purpose of a Media Room is to post any and all items so members of the media might go looking for it to help them do their jobs! The easier you make it for them to find interview questions, your biography, photos, press releases, write-ups and articles, the easier it will be for them to say, "When can we do the interview!"

What sections make up a great Media Room?

A great Media Room must have some, if not all, of the following sections so the media can pick and choose what they need to help them help you with the interview.

1. **About (You, Your Website, Business or Product/Service)** ... Here's a section that either tells a little bit about you, or a lot, or links to your About Us page on your website. When members of the media come to your Media Room and want more information about you and your company, product, etc., they'll look for this section and quickly gain an understanding "about" who you are and much more.

2. **Articles, Stories & Write-Ups** ... Do you write articles? You don't have to list them in this section, but you might link to the article section on your website inside your Media Room. Articles give members of the media ideas for their own shows. If you wrote an article that inspires them to interview you, make sure they know where to find them on your site. Link to your articles section within your Media Room.

3. **Awards & Recognitions** ... Have you received any awards or recognition for what you do? Make sure you post a section within your Media Room that highlights these accomplishments.

4. **Biography Information** ... Who are you? Make it easy for members of the media to learn about you. Post your bio in your Media Room, or at least link to it. Also, make your bio available via PDF so they can print it from your website and read it on air or make notes for a TV introduction if you're ever interviewed in that manner.

5. **Highlights & Special Announcements** ... Do you often make announcements to your list of clients, prospects and affiliates about new products, services, etc.? Post these announcements in your Media Room for the media to see. Remember, members of the media are hungry for information about you, what's going on in your world, etc. So, be sure to create a section in your Media Room that lists any new announcements you might make.

6. **Facts 'N Figures** ... Are there any particular facts and figures you might want potential members of the media or other visitors to your website to know about your company, your earnings, stock market performances, etc.? Then post those "facts 'n figures" under a section called Facts & Figures or Fact Sheets or something similar.

7. **Images / Photo Gallery** ... This is a must-have section to include in your Media Room. When members of the media want to interview you, or other people want to do a review of your products/services, send them to your Media Room where they can download web-ready or high resolution images of you, your products, book covers ... you name it. Typically, you should provide a 72 dpi (for web use) and a 300 dpi (for print use) quality image for every image you provide inside your Media Room's image gallery area.

8. **Interview (Your Name)** ... Another must-have section of your Media Room, is the "Interview Your Name" section. Why not personalize this section if you can. When members of the media go looking through your Media Room and see a section called "Interview Bart Smith" immediately, they might just be inclined to pick up the phone and call you. At a minimum, it motivates them to ... "interview you!" Inside this section, you can list ways to contact you, in addition to a list of questions they can ask you about what it is you do, your book, company, etc. Again, it's a must-have section for your Media Room.

9. **Interview Questions & Talking Points** ... It's another must-have section to be included in your Media Room. It makes it easy for members of the media and others to interview you. Create a list of questions or "talking points" and make those questions available on your website. You can either list the questions on their own page, and/or

provide a download link to a PDF allowing someone to download and print the questions on their computer for easy reference when they interview you.

10. **Investor Relations** ... Are you looking for investment capital to fund your growing business? Mention it inside your Media Room. Let people know you're looking for investors with x-amount of capital to invest in x-projects. You don't have to go into specifics here, but sometimes a simple statement mentioning you're looking for investors will suffice. You might also list certain documents and references to stock market numbers that might help encourage a prospective investor to pick up the phone and call you for more information.

11. **Latest News** ... What's new? What's the latest development happening in your business? Did you come up with a new product? Did you attend (or plan to) a seminar or other networking event? Tell folks about the latest and greatest happenings in your world in your Media Room.

12. **Media Contact Information** ... This section is a must-have area on your website that gives members of the media and others information as to who they should contact to discuss matters relating to your website, publicity, public relations, the media, interviews and anything else mentioned in your Media Room. If you have a separate phone number for your media contact, encourage customers, affiliates and prospects not to call that number. Explain that it's for "MEDIA ONLY".

13. **Networking & Sightings** ... Will you be attending a networking event, seminar, workshop or other type of event soon? List it inside your Media Room under a section called, "Sites & Appearances". This section serves a couple purposes: (1) It lets people know where you'll be so they can attend the same event in hopes of meeting you. (2) When you attend

these events, you're going to take pictures, right? Of course you will! Take those pictures and post them in your Media Room. When you do, and people look through them and they're from the media, you can bet they're saying to themselves, "Wow, this person is really active, out there, and making a name for himself/herself. I need to invite that person to be a guest on my show. Talk about a great guest!"

14. **News & Media Coverage ("In The News")** ... Are you being discussed in the media? GREAT! Link to those websites that talk about you, grab their corporate logo and post all of them in your Media Room. Sign up for Google Alerts, which will send you eMail updates whenever your personal name, product, company name is ever mentioned on the Web.

15. **Newsletter Sign-up** ... If you have a online newsletter or ezine, why not make it easy for members of the media and others to subscribe to it. This is a great way for them to join your list and get to know what you're all about. If you need the ability to do this, sign up for **Sender.net**, which has eMail broadcasting, eZine delivery and the ability to create opt-in boxes to collect the name and eMail from people wanting to subscribe to your online newsletter. You can also list past issues of your eZine in your Media Room, too. Remember, members of the media and others like them are always looking for information and material to report on. Reading your eZine articles might initiate an idea for them to pick up the phone and call you!

16. **Podcasting Shows** ... Do you have your own podcast show? No? Why not! Yes, good for you! If you do have your own radio show online, why not post a link to those recordings and/or how to listen to future podcast shows. If you don't know what a podcast show is, check out my tutorial at **BartSmith.com/ training** called, **Create Your Own Podcast Show.**

17. **Media Kit** ... This is the online version of a regular Media kit you would normally send out through the U.S. mail to someone who requests it. Members of the media who are interested in interviewing you, having you on their show or get to know you better will request a Media kit. Depending on the kind of industry you're in, you might have any one of the following items included in your Media kit: Media release about you or your book or product, a photo of yourself, a copy of your book, a list of interview questions, video of other interviews or speaking, two business cards and anything else you think would be of interest to the media. Now, fast forward to today! With the Internet, you have the ability to place many of these items online! Who needs to mail anymore? Video can be viewed online, interview questions downloaded, images copied and saved to one's computer for their use, etc. So, build a section in your Media Room with your Media kit already available.

18. **Press Releases** ... Press releases are newsworthy, one-page announcements about you, your book, a new joint venture, or other news event written by you (or someone you hire) for distribution by the media. Press releases are not advertisements. Rather, they are written to "inform." Depending on how busy you are with what you do, you should be posting at least one new press release to your Media Room per a week.

19. **Product Information, Reviews or Synopsis** ... Again, make it easy for people to find information about what you do. If you sell products or provide services, provide quick links to these pages in your Media Room. When someone's skimming your Media Room and discovers you offer x-products and services, they just might click on the respective link(s). Doing so might encourage them to pick up the phone and contact you to talk more with them.

20. **TV/Radio Interviews (Previously Recorded)** ... Were you on TV or the radio? Were you able to record any of those shows? If so, place them in your Media room for people to listen to. If a potential interviewer hears you being interviewed on other stations, what do you think their confidence level will be when they decide to call you for an interview? Pretty high, eh? You bet!

21. **Rave Reviews** ... What do others say about what you do? Provide a quick link within your Media Room to your testimonial or rave reviews page. When potential interviewers want to interview you and see all your testimonials, they'll think, "Wow, if these people liked this person's x-product/y-service, there's a good chance my audience will too. Let's see, where's their phone number?"

22. **Reports (Annual Report, Financial Report, etc.)** ... Do you have financial information you need to share with people to help them make a decision to work or invest with you? Then, upload those documents to your website and mention them in your Media Room.

23. **Social Networking Profiles** ... Do you have a Facebook fan page or group? Instagram? TikTok? X? LinkedIn page? List all the social networking sites you're linked on from within your Media Room. People who want to learn more about you, would also like to check out your social networking pages and connect with you there.

24. **Speaking & Seminar Coverage** ... Do you conduct tele-seminars, seminars or other speaking events? Provide a link within your Media Room to your speaking calendar. People skimming through your Media Room might see that you speak and might want to try to attend one (or more) of your speaking events, if possible. Others might

want to hire you and here's a great place for them to find out such information, inside your Media Room.

25. **Upcoming Events** … Are you speaking soon? Going to an event? Putting on an event? Tell people about it inside your Media Room. Again, this is the area of your website that represents you and what you're doing NOW! If you let people know where you'll be, they might be encouraged to attend with hopes of meeting you. Getting photographs you can place in your Media Room photo gallery with those who support and respect what you do really speaks volumes about you as a person.

26. **Video Presentations & Coverage** … Do you have videos on your website, YouTube.com or other video sharing websites? Were you seen on television? Can you find that video on the Internet and link to it from within your Media Room? This is another great place for you to showcase all the video work you've been doing. Create a section in your Media Room where you either showcase the few videos you have or link to a web page where you keep all of your videos.

You can imagine again how confident you'd be if you had a section like this on your website before you launched out looking for interviews. Not that it's a must-have on your website, but I know you see the importance of having a Media Room on your website.

As you accumulate a track record of interviews, showcase them inside your media room to boost more confidence in future show hosts and producers about *booking you in a flash for their next show.*

PART 4

Do You Have
Any Pre-Recorded
**Sample Interviews
Of You On Video**
On Your Website?

TVGuest.com

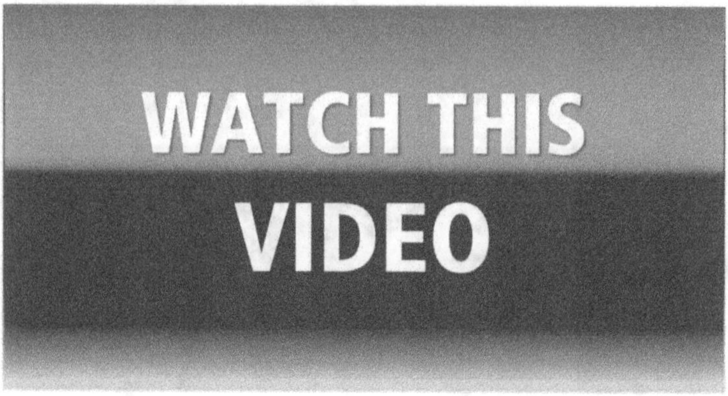
WATCH THIS
VIDEO

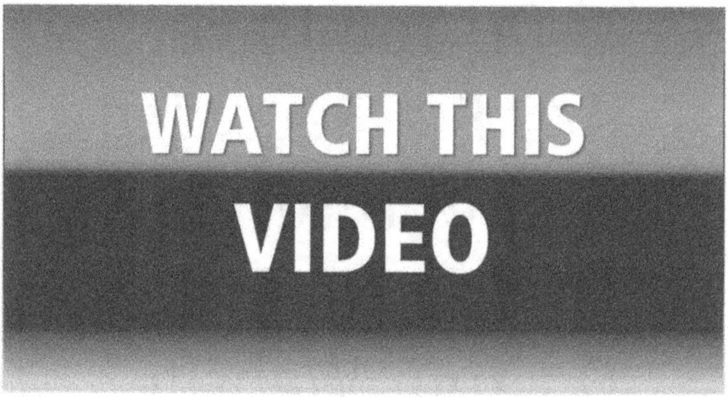
WATCH THIS
VIDEO

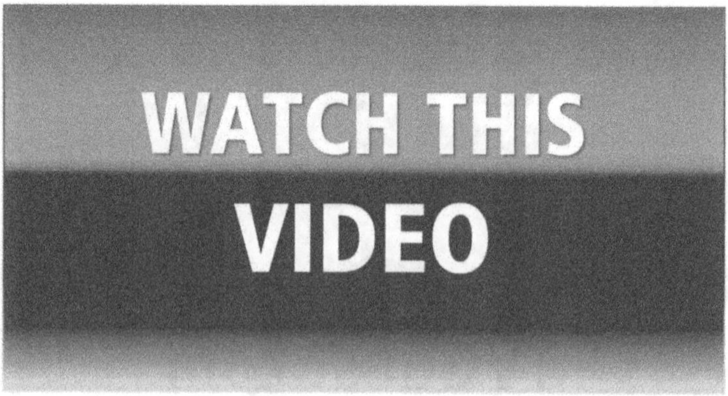
WATCH THIS
VIDEO

What are sample interviews on video?

These are simply videos of you in actual interviews or sample ones to help impress show hosts to interview you based on what they saw and heard in those video interviews that you created and posted on your website, in your media room, or on pages that benefit from you having a sample interview video on them.

These video interviews can last anywhere between 5-25 minutes or longer if you choose. Ideally, the shorter, the better. For example, you might decide to film yourself answering 3-5 of the top most pressing questions you enjoy answering or your entire list of 10-20 questions found on your "Interview Me" page.

It's up to you. Some folks will watch the whole video for their own personal enjoyment or for a learning opportunity about what you do or have to say.

Why do you need sample interviews on video?

There are a couple of reasons. For starters, these sample interview videos can introduce you and expand on what you are promoting or the message you want to get across to people. For example, you might have a book you want to promote. Well, just don't post strictly sales copy on your website to sell your book. Readers want to know about you, the author.

Create a video trailer for the book itself and a video recording of you getting interviewed about your book. Give potential buyers of your product/service a real inside look into why you wrote/created the book, what you do and how folks can benefit from reading it. With you in the video, it has more power to convince and sell folks to buy your book vs. reading flat sales copy.

Another great reason to create a video with you being interviewed is to make it extremely fast and easy so show hosts will say, "Wow, I like how you answered those interview questions and you looked great on camera! I'm very excited to interview you, too. My audience is going to love you and what you have to say regarding the topics you cover so well." Need I say more?

You see, many hosts are inundated with requests from people to get interviewed. To stand out among the competition, provide a real life sample video of you being interviewed. Inspire hosts to choose you over hundreds of others because your video moved them!

What is an example of an interview video?

On my websites, **MyTrainingCenter.com**, **BartSmith.com** and **TVGuest.com**, you'll find a few examples of video interviews I recorded for prospective show hosts and interview decision makers to preview before contacting me with an invitation to be interviewed on their shows.

What's more, anyone can watch these and learn about x-topic before making a buying decision. *"Wow, I really liked how he answered those questions. I'm curious to see what else he covers in his book."* You get the idea.

You'll be able to get a lot of ideas for recording your own (sample) interviews on video by watching mine. Use whatever you like for your own video.

How do you create these interviews on video?

To be honest, do this:

1. **Find a nice, clean area in your home/office** to set up a clean and simple environment for filming with you on video for a few minutes.

2. **Setup some professional lights** so you're well-lit in your videos. Buy these on Amazon for under $100.

3. **Setup your phone on a 72" tripod to film you.** I'd link a lavalier microphone to your phone to enhance the quality of the audio being recorded in your video.

4. **Print out a list of questions in large print on a sheet of paper** that you can keep by your side as a ready reference. "Okay, the next question I'll answer is ..."

5. **OPTIONAL: Film each answer to x-question in a separate video on your phone.** You're going to piece them together later in one long video in post-production.

6. **ANOTHER OPTION: Go ahead and film one long video with you answering all your questions** and then just cut/edit the video in post-production.

7. **Display a series of different emotions in your answers:** seriousness, laughter, smiles, minimize hand waving, keep your posture sitting straight upright with shoulders back and head held upright, etc.

8. **When done, transfer all those videos off your phone** to your computer for editing.

9. **Open up your editing program,** import all the videos, place them on the time line and piece them together.

10. **Insert a black space with white text**, between each question you answer, displaying the question you are

about to answer beforehand.

11. **Insert any other text in the intro/outro** of your video, perhaps stating what the interview is about.

12. **DONE. Publish it, review it, make changes** and then if you like it upload it to your website (where it belongs) and/or to video sharing websites.

In a nutshell, these are the steps to create a simple video interview with you answering a few key questions. Once you make one of these videos, make a few more for other books you wrote, products/services you'd like people to know more about, etc.

Need help with this?

If you do, ask around to get someone to help you. Make it a fun project for an afternoon. Set aside about 2-3 hours for this (or more) and perhaps take your assistant to lunch/dinner or pay them $50 for his/her time, which will be appreciated.

Once you get the hang of it, you'll probably want to answer different questions in a different video and in a different setting. Go for it. Keep shooting video of yourself until you have the best video filmed for a specific interview segment. That's what I do. You can do it, too!

PART 5

Learn How To Get
"Author Interviews"
For The Book
You Just Wrote

TVGuest.com

SO, YOU JUST WROTE A NEW BOOK and you're excited to share it with the world. Well, one of the best ways to do that is to get interviewed by people who have their own podcast/ radio/TV show, website, forum, blog, newsletter/eZine and an audience ready to consume what you've just written. Getting your book in front of audiences will do wonders for you when it comes to making book sales, exposure for your services, a boost to your credibility, pave the way for getting more interviews, even approached by publishing companies who can help take your book to the next level, as well as your overall success as an author.

Getting interviews is one of the fastest, cheapest and most efficient ways to get your book out there. Today, there are literally thousands of online radio shows, blogs, websites and even TV shows that would like to interview you if your book's content/message is a good fit for their show. The number of interviews you could go after is only limited by your own efforts and/or those you hire to help you find and secure interviews.

In this section, you'll learn exactly how to get an unlimited number of interviews. Here are a number of questions to quickly ask yourself that I'll also answer in the section below. But, here's the basic MIND SET when it comes to getting interviews for you and your book:

1. **What do you want to be interviewed about?** What's the subject matter?

2. **Are you prepared to give an interview?** There's a lot that goes into preparation and I'll discuss that upcoming.

3. **How well do you know** your own material?

4. **How do you go about finding** interview opportunities?

Get A Profile Listing On TVGuest.com & Get More Interviews

5. **To find interview opportunities on your own**, follow these procedures …

6. **Stay organized as you search** for and accumulate interview opportunities.

7. **At this point, all you need to do now is** review my INTERVIEW CHECKLIST.

Having read over this short list, let's dive into each of them below in more detail with the "what-to/how-to" knowledge you'll need to get interviewed.

1. What do you want to be interviewed about? What's the subject matter?

Naturally, this is an easy question, your book, of course. BUT, what's important to know is whatever your book's subject matter is about, you'll be chasing after similar, like-minded podcast/radio shows, websites and blog owners whose audience will be interested in your book's topic.

In the beginning, go for niche interviews, as I call them. Focus on your niche, and go after those shows, websites and blogs whose audiences are a perfect match for your subject. Exhaust your research finding up to 100 different interview opportunities where your book's subject matter is a perfect match.

After many interviews, other shows and websites who you would have never approached just might seek you out because they heard you and want to have you as a guest on their show even though (at first glance) you never would have thought to approach them, and they you, until you actually invested in all those interviews.

2. Are you prepared to give an interview?

There's a lot that goes into preparing to do interviews about your book, such as ...

(a) Do you have interview questions ready to hand over to the person you want to interview you with the click of your mouse? Generate about 10 questions for the interviewer to ask that you can answer with ease and confidence. Help them do their job (i.e., interviewing you) by providing them with questions about your book. You can see sample questions that I've come up with about my books to get ideas for your own questions. Just check out:

BartSmith.com/interviews

(b) Do you have a press room or media page on your website where you can post these questions? This way, all you have to do is send this web link to the interviewer to get the information they need in order to conduct the interview. If you have more than one book you want to be interviewed for, be sure to create separate interview pages for each book. On these pages, you might include images/artwork about you and your book, interview questions, your bio, how to introduce you, how to order your book, how to schedule an interview, sample interviews if you have them, and suggested interviews if you have other books. For example, check out this page where I have what most interviewers might need to use.

(c) Do you have 150-300 dpi (high-resolution) images of you and your book's front cover? These are essential to have so the interviewer can display them on their website or on their actual show.

(d) Is your website ready to take orders? Is your shopping

cart tested? Is your payment gateway ready to receive thousands of dollars in orders within an hour's period (pray that happens) and it won't be shut off by your merchant account company because they think there's some sort of fraudulent ordering going on? PayPal, for example, doesn't have this problem. They won't turn off your ability to accept thousands of dollars in orders in any given period. Whereas, companies like Authorize.net, and similar merchant providers will turn you off until you contact them to inform them on what's going on.

Further, they may even hold your incoming funds for 90 days. OUCH! That would certainly put a dent in your ability to purchase supplies and inventory to fill those orders. Either way, check with your payment gateway or merchant account provider and ask them, "If I generate a high volume of sales within a very short time, such as a single day or two, how will you respond (if you will at all)? Will you turn off my ability to accept large orders? Will you hold my funds for a certain period of time? What do you do when there's a SPIKE in orders, because I'll be doing interviews and I just might get a few hundred orders within a day or week's time." If they say, "Yes, we typically would shut you off or at least hold your funds for 30 days ...," then you have your answer and REASON TO LEAVE THEM.

These companies do this only to protect themselves against charge-backs and fraudulent purchases, which in your case, isn't the case hopefully because all you did was generate high exposure for your book and a number of people bought it because of the show. Your orders are from legit customers who want your book and are willing to pay you with real money. So, keep this very important point in mind BEFORE you set out to conduct interviews.

(e) How will you handle fulfillment of your book? Suppose you receive 50 or 5,000 orders in a single day from one interview? How would you fill them? Manually? Use a fulfillment company? Drop ship them one by one using your printer if your account has that functionality. Depending on the audience(s) you interview and the size of it, your choice of fulfillment procedures should match that. For example, if your rate of return on your interviews on a monthly basis runs about 10-100 book sales, you can fulfill those yourself or use a drop-ship service through your book printer.

If you generate 100+ orders per month, then you might consider sending all your traffic to an online retailer like Amazon.com to transact all the sales (at any volume) and fulfill those orders through their warehouse. Leave all that work to them while you work on interviews, promotion and collecting royalties for all your efforts.

3. How well do you know your own material?

This sounds basic, but it's so true. When put on the spot, how well DO you know your own material? For starters, create a list of 10 questions that you'd like to be asked regarding your book and then REHEARSE REHEARSE REHEARSE. Practice answering those questions with confidence at least 30-45 minutes a day until you have the answers down pat.

Grab a friend and ask him/her to ask you those questions. Pretend you're actually being interviewed. This rehearsal can be done in person, over the telephone or over Skype. What's more, dedicate one of your books to be used exclusively for interviews. That is, this book will always be by your side during interviews. In this specific book, you might place little notes and tabs in the book where your questions are referenced. JUST IN CASE you need to quickly reference the answer to a question being asked, you have it marked in your book by a tab or bookmark. Keep this book in a safe place because you'll use it often with all your interviews.

Another good idea is to listen to your interviews after they've been rehearsed and conducted. Doing so will help you pick up on great things you've said and any mistakes made. Make notes of the mistakes you made and the good points you said in your interviews so you get better as you go along with every interview you do.

Do you need to brush up on your material for your next interview? Go back and listen to one your previously recorded interviews. You did put your past recorded interviews on your web page for easy access and listening for potential future interviewers, right?

4. How do you go about finding interview opportunities?

Once you have your questions, web page with interview information for the interviewer, you're rehearsed and your fulfillment and payment situations are in place and prepared, it's time to start looking for interview opportunities. Now, there are essentially a couple of ways to go about getting interviews:

PAY TO GET THEM: You could approach certain publicity firms that already have relationships with radio and TV shows and they will get you on those shows to be interviewed. The problem with that, to some degree, is:

This can be expensive — anywhere between $500 to $5,000 per month. It all depends on the company you're using and what kind of interviews they get you. Are they radio interviews where the audience runs between 500,000 to 5,000,000? Are they TV interviews where viewership could run as high as 10,000,000? Would it be worth the investment? Sure, if you could sell 1,000 books per interview with audiences that large. Do you have a media budget set aside for this? It's best to have between $2,500 and $5,000 if you're going to go this route to get you started. Do note, it's not necessary to take this approach in the beginning. Only if you have the kind of publicity budget set aside and you're in a hurry to get BIG EXPOSURE quickly and then you go for it!

For MOST (new) authors, it's not always a good idea to get interviewed in front of such large audiences. Don't waste the opportunity and blow it because you didn't have your ducks in order to monetize exposure of that magnitude. Instead, it's recommended that you get your feet wet by conducting 20-30 smaller interviews. In the beginning, most authors are new to the whole interview process. With so many aspects to be polished and ironed out, it's best to find interviews where your audiences range between 2,500 and 25,000.

Here are some websites to get you started and their fees are reasonable to get the kind of exposure you need to attract interviews. If you go to these sites, they can offer you opportunities to list yourself as an available guest.

- **RadioGuestList.com**
- **RadioGuest.com**
- **InterviewGuestsDirectory.com**
- **MediaGuestConnect.com**
- **TVGuest.com** (*Bart's TV/Radio Guest Directory!*)

There are more sites just like the above. Do a little research, you'll get ideas to help you branch out and find similar websites to list yourself as a interview guest on several sites.

Get A Profile Listing On TVGuest.com & Get More Interviews

FIND THEM YOURSELF (FREE/JUST TAKES TIME): There are literally thousands of online radio shows, websites, and blogs who would love to interview you for their show. There is no shortage of interview opportunities out there. YOU just have to go after them. Don't hesitate. You'll be amazed to find out how grateful many of these hosts are that you have searched them out. You're a breath of fresh air to many because they're always looking for fresh content and guests to share their perspectives on their expertise.

5. To find interview opportunities on your own, follow these procedures!

Using your favorite search engine, like Google, perform several online searches for podcast shows, online radio shows, talk radio, satellite radio, and TV talk show websites, businesses and blogs that align with your book's subject matter. For example, "relationship podcast shows" or "relationship blogs" or "relationship advice websites." You get the idea. Again, there are hundreds, if not thousands, so don't say you can't find any. You're just not searching hard or long enough. Give it a week's worth of searching to see how many prospects you can come up with to approach for an interview. Make a list of at least 20, if not 50, interview opportunities to approach about interviewing you.

Remember, all it takes is a little time, some good ol' persistence and patience, and you'll find the right sites for you. For example, if you wrote a relationship book, you might contact dating websites, relationship blogs, online magazines, advice websites, relationship podcast shows, and the like. By doing so, now, you've got 100's of potential interviews just waiting for you. If you only scored 10 interviews in the next 30 days based on those 100 opportunities, that's great! Ten interviews soon leads to 10 more and then 20 and then there is no limit to the number of interviews you can develop.

Once you find them, search the websites for a web page dedicated to their show. On that page, look for a link that says something like "BE A GUEST" or similar. Seriously, it's that simple. When you find it, click on the link and submit your inquiry about why you would be a great guest on their show and then wait for a reply. Typically, they'll respond within 24-72 hours. If not, follow up within a week. Once they reply, you can discuss the potential for interviewing on their shows and decide whether they will or will not meet your needs.

If they don't have such a page, or you can't find a "BE A GUEST" (or similar) link, then simply send them a inquiry through their Contact Us page. Usually, they have an online contact form on their Contact Us page. I've done this before with success. If you happen to find out who the producer or host of the show is, use their name in the letter you'll be sending them in the contact form.

Customize and send the following letter in their website's online Contact Us form:

SUBJECT:
New Guest For Your Show | (YOUR NICHE) Expert/Author

Dear (Producer's Name),

I'm writing to inquire about being a guest on your next show! The next time you do a show/story on (YOUR BOOK'S TOPIC/SUBJECT MATTER THAT RELATES TO THEIR SHOW), please consider me.

My name is (YOUR NAME), and I'm the author of (BOOK TITLE), and I'm a (BOOK'S TOPIC/SUBJECT) expert and can give insightful/credible commentary when you need a guest expert on this topic.

You can learn more about my book here:
(INSERT LINK, DO NOT ATTACH A FILE)

(IF YOU HAVE PREVIOUS INTERVIEW EXPERIENCE) I've been on radio and TV several times, and feel very comfortable conducting interviews. You can listen to my past interviews here: (INSERT LINK)

I'm based in (YOUR CITY/STATE). I can be available for your show if given an hour's notice, otherwise, we can schedule an interview when you need a guest expert for your show.

My bio is located at my website, YourSite.com/about, and if I can ever be of any help to you in the future, please feel free to reach out.

All the best,

 Your Full Name
(000) 000-0000 (Cell/Text)
eMail Address
Website URL

While you wait for their reply, send out 5-10 more interview inquiries that day to other shows/websites. Try sending out 10-20 interview inquiries per week until you start to fill up your calendar with replies and scheduled interviews. Then, minimize the number of inquiries you send out to focus on delivering quality interviewing on shows scheduled. When you're wrapping up your scheduled interviews, start looking for some new ones to add to your calendar. If you hear something come up in the news and you have or have not heard back from those you sent interview inquiries to, reach out to them with an eMail through their Contact Us form that reads:

SUBJECT:
Expert For You Regarding (Topic In The News That Relates To Your Expertise)

Dear (Producer's Name),

If you need an expert on (YOUR TOPIC), I've written a book on (YOUR TOPIC AS IT RELATES TO WHAT'S GOING ON IN THE NEWS) and am available for interviews.

(USE THIS SECOND SENTENCE HERE TO COMMENT OR PROVIDE YOUR PERSPECTIVE ON THE ITEM IN THE NEWS. THEY WILL READ THIS AND MAKE THE CALL TO BOOK YOU AS A GUEST IF THEY LIKE WHAT THEY READ AND IT APPLIES TO THEM WELL.)

I'd be happy to help you and your guests gain a brighter perspective on this topic. I can share with your audience what I talk about in my book and how I advise my clients.

Best Regards,

Your Full Name
Cell Number
eMail
Website URL

That's it. This is how you'll stay in touch with shows, hosts, producers, websites and blog owners who you'd like to get interviewed by. Keep at it, don't let up, don't be bothersome, but don't let yourself be forgotten either. It's a number's game out there. Play the numbers. For every 10 interview inquiries you send out, you're bound to get 2-3 back who want to interview you soon, with another 2-5 right behind them after they read your eMail. Those are pretty good numbers when you consider there are thousands of interview opportunities out there, today. So? Go after those 100+ shows who will book you!

6. Stay organized as you search for and accumulate interview opportunities.

While there are several ways to stay organized as you hunt down interview opportunities, one very unique way to do this follows:

CALENDAR SYSTEM:

You'll need a calendar system, such as Google Calendar, to post and keep track of all your upcoming interviews. Times, dates, name of show, their website, etc. These calendar entries will send you helpful reminders about the date/time of the interview. Once you enter the interview event in your calendar, make notes for this show in some sort of CONTACT MANAGEMENT DATABASE.

CONTACT MANAGEMENT DATABASE:

I created a GROUP inside my Google Contacts in which to document all kinds of information regarding the interview I'm about to conduct. I can also make detailed notes about the radio show, their website, the people who work there, special instructions, and so much more. All of this is very handy when it comes to staying organized and booking a ton of interviews for you.

7. It's ALMOST time to review my INTERVIEW CHECKLISTS!

Yes, soon, what you'll need to do is to review (PART 7) INTERVIEW CHECKLIST for how-to/what-to instruction as it relates to these hot topics below:

1.0 – Prepare For The Perfect Interview

2.0 – How To Get A Radio Interview

3.0 – What To Do Before The Interview

4.0 – Recording Interviews

5.0 – Media Interview Techniques

6.0 – What To Send Prior To The Interview

7.0 – Plugging Your Own Book, Product, Service Or Website

8.0 – What To Do After The Interview

PART 6

Here Are **10 Ways** You Can **Personally Improve Your Interview Skills** So You Come Across As A Seasoned **"Professional Interviewer"** Every Time!

TVGuest.com

WHEN IT COMES TO MARKETING AND GETTING EXPOSURE FOR YOUR BOOK/PRODUCT/SERVICES/BUSINESS, the more interviews you can give to website owners, podcast shows, magazines, newspapers, eZine publishers, social media influencers, YouTube video channel owners, radio talk show hosts, TV talk show hosts, you name it, the better to enhance your career, business, bank account and your *interviewing skills!*

When it comes to giving those interviews and being interviewed, you MUST be ready. How do you prepare? Simple! Follow these 10 EASY WAYS TO IMPROVE YOUR INTERVIEW SKILLS and you'll be ready to approach and secure all the interviews you can get!

INTERVIEW **TIP** #1

Listen closely to other people being interviewed on radio, online, TV and pay attention to what's asked and HOW they respond. Listen and watch for the good, the bad and the ugly!

Yes, actively listen to people who are interviewed on the radio, online, on podcast shows, TV shows, etc. Listen and learn. The more you hear other interviewees, the more you'll learn and the more comfortable you'll feel when it's your turn to get behind the microphone for an interview.

Listen to short and long interviews, and play along with the host as if you're the one being interviewed. To prepare for short and long interviews, have a list of 6-12 questions, even a longer list of questions (i.e., 24-48 questions), so you're prepared for any length of interview.

Can you learn anything from how others respond to their interviews? Absolutely! Are they prepared? To the degree they "perform" in front of the microphone/camera, you, too, need to match their performance even excel! Interviewing is a performance; don't forget that. You are providing the "entertainment" when you're interviewed. So, you too, have to connect with the audience and not just the person interviewing you. Give them, with great answers, a smile, laughter, the "real you" and something to remember you by. You're the guest (of honor) on their show, so, get excited!

What do people who get interviewed SAY? HOW do they respond? Do they appear nervous, uneasy, uncomfortable, pressured, angered (by the interviewer), excited, happy? Do not allow the interviewer to agitate you or make you angry. KEEP YOUR HEAD throughout the interview. Never raise your voice, never shout and never talk over other guests or the host, and never ever .... lose your cool. Stay calm throughout, even if you don't get the chance to speak, because there are other guests who may be losing control. Don't let it be you!

Show the mature side of you and always keep it cool. After the interview is over, what will people walk away knowing? They saw that you were in control while others, possibly, were NOT! No matter what your position is on a topic, people respect people who are always in control of their emotions. Maintain control always! You'll make more inroads when you can manage your emotions and stay calm under pressure. Notice how others come across? Do they sound/look good/bad? You might only be on the air for five minutes (maybe longer) ... give your best performance and you'll be remembered for how you composed yourself, your quick/intelligent responses, positive energy, etc.

Learn from others and don't repeat the bad, only the good. Seriously, if you see someone say something YOU thought about saying, or could SEE YOURSELF SAYING, but you saw how the host and/or audience reacted (negatively) to it then don't say it! Strike it off your "can't say" list when giving interviews or reword it so it leaves a positive impression versus a negative one.

Sometimes, you can pick up certain catch phrases or soundbites listening to others being interviewed, which you can use in your own interviews. Listening to others being interviewed also educates you on a variety of topics and subjects. Watching and learning can turn you into a great interviewee and TV guest!

INTERVIEW **TIP** #2

Listen to the host or person conducting the interview asking all the questions for these tips ...

You can learn a lot about the interviewing process by listening to hosts on a number of different shows and their interview styles. How do they introduce guests, run their shows, ask questions, transition to breaks for ads, bring back the show/interviewee (you) into the conversation again.

If you are going to be on a particular show or would like to be interviewed on a specific show, here's a great tip to ensure your success for (1) getting it and (2) being interviewed on the show. Ready? LISTEN TO 10+ PAST SHOWS where they interviewed a guest so you can learn more about the host's style for interviewing guests. When you can get a feel for that host and how they operate, you can better help them to interview you.

Get familiar with different style formats; single guest (i.e., you), multiple guests, multiple hosts, etc. By doing this, you'll get comfortable with these formats and won't be surprised by any of them. Listen to a variety of interviews to get comfortable with the formats. Study them and master them. Specifically, how are they asking questions? Are they friendly or antagonistic and likely to produce/generate some form of controversy (with you) to help boost their show's ratings?

Choose, ahead of time, if you'd like to be interviewed in a positive light or if you're strong enough to go into the jungle and be interviewed by someone only interested in boosting ratings by placing you on the spot and in hot situations that might only agitate you and not really bring out the best in you for their audience.

Why take on a tough interview like that? For exposure? To set the record straight, if you have something to say about a certain topic, pass on negative comments and only take on positive interviews. Up to you!

Your press room will thank you for keeping cool. Be prepared to be interviewed by all kinds of people. Imagine yourself being interviewed by a particular host. How would you respond to their questions? Practice how you'd respond to pressing questions or comments that push your buttons.

INTERVIEW **TIP** #3

Watch others being interviewed on TV and on the Internet often ...

What can you learn by WATCHING other people's interviews? A LOT! You learn what to wear and what not to wear; how to respond and how not to respond; how to sit/stand and how not to among other attributes to giving live, in-person, video-recorded interviews for television or distribution on the Internet.

Watch how the person being interviewed composes themselves physically. Do they lean forward, sway side to side when responding to questions or do they close their eyes when answering them?

When it comes to your eyes, keep them open and on target (looking at the host, camera or the audience from time to time). Be mindful of your posture when giving answers. How you hold yourself together can be interpreted as not being truthful or sincere and people may not believe or respect you when answering uncomfortable questions.

Are the guests groomed well? Honestly, if you're ever interviewed on television or other video outlet, look your best! Look sharp, well-groomed, well-rested. It's hard to look relaxed when you're nervous, so dress for success, as they say.

If you must, get help with your attire, but always look your very best! Before you open your mouth, people will judge you based on your image and how you carry yourself on screen and in front of an audience.

INTERVIEW TIP #4

Record your own interviews and learn from them ...

Absolutely! Record all your interviews and post them on your website's press room, social media channels, video channels, and more. AFTER the interview, edit some of the front and back end of the audio so your listeners get to the meat right away. Feel free to edit out the commercials, too. I do. There are a number of services and phone apps you can use to record telephone interviews. You can also ask the host to give you the name of the producer to see if they'll give you a copy of the interview via MP3 download.

If you're going to be interviewed live in front of a video camera (for a live televised show), know the date it will air and get ready to record it if you have the means. Otherwise, many shows air online, too, where you can simply look for an embed code if they provide one so you can place the video on your website. When you record every interview, you can listen to them and learn from them. What did you say that you won't ever say again? What did you say that you'd like to use in future interviews? Write them down, make notes, and make every interview, from this point and going forward, your best ever!

INTERVIEW **TIP** #5

Know your topic inside and out and be excited about telling your story ...

When you know your topic of expertise inside and out, you interview well because you have a ton of information you can turn into answers at every corner (i.e., question) of the interview. Be able to introduce yourself, what you do, and your topic in short concise answers. "Yes, well I do _____ and help _____, so they _____."

Read, read, read everything you can about your topic of expertise. Always, be continually learning and gaining new insights, facts, figures, etc., which you can use in your interviews. Attend seminars, lectures and workshops on your topic of expertise. Again, keep information on your topic fresh so people look forward to your interviews. Become an expert in your field. The more you know about your topic of expertise, the more interviews you can get. See how that works? Also, write out 5-10 questions and their answers and then print them so you can read them over and over, again. You could also record the questions and your answers and listen to it over and over. For a longer interview, write out 10-20 questions and their answers. Again, print out the questions and answers and practice, practice, practice. Have you ever listened to speakers who for all appearances didn't know what they were talking about? Be prepared, rehearsed and know your subject inside and out!

INTERVIEW **TIP** #6

Don't talk on and on even though you were asked a question that requires a long, detailed answer ...

When asked a question, give a brief, yet, detailed response. Don't overdue it with fact after fact after fact. Remember, there are two people in this interview; you and the host. It's a two-way street and you need to allow the interviewer to ask more questions. This doesn't mean one-word answers, either. Never respond with one word answers. If the answer to their question is "yes" or "no", then say so, but add a pertinent comment to the "yes" or "no" response .... "Yes, because if you ...." . Always remember, the interviewer wants to get as much information as possible for the benefit of his/her audience. The interviewer won't ask two questions and then turn the microphone over to you. It's not your show. They ask the questions; you answer them. Be considerate and give the interviewer plenty of room to ask their questions by ending your answers after a few seconds of response. Sure, you might have more to add, but don't. Leave the audience wanting more, and let the host ask you a new question that gives you an opportunity to say more. Let the process work for you. If you try to steal the show, trust me, they'll never ask you back!

INTERVIEW **TIP** #7

Have your "freebie" ready and be excited to share it ...

Don't get interviewed by everyone you can for the sake of being interviewed. Your goal for interviewing should be to grow your business and your list of new prospects besides building credibility and demand for what you have to offer over the course of your career!

The way you build your list of prospects, when interviewing, is to invite your listening audience to take advantage of a "freebie" you're offering during the interview. "Yes, you can get free excerpts of my new book at my website, MyWebsite.com." Or, "Get my free report on xyz _____ at my website, go to MyWebsite.com." Or, "Call 1-800-000-0000 to get your free _____!"

When you're interviewed, you have the ability to reach hundreds, perhaps thousands of people who really admire and enjoy the hosts who are interviewing you. If you're on their shows, most likely, there's a good chance, your audience will like you, too. So? Have a freebie ready to give to audiences. This could be in the form of a free report, eZine/newsletter, audio program, book excerpt, a free tele-call, a free webinar, a free trial of one your products or services.

Whatever you do, don't offer anything that might cost you money, unless you're giving something away to only a few "winners!" Otherwise, come up with a digital giveaway that you can give to the masses for listening to your interview.

INTERVIEW TIP #8

Have your "special offer" primed, polished and ready to share in as few words as possible ...

In addition to having your "freebie" ready to help build your list of prospects who you can sell to later, you should also plan to have a "special offer" you can give to the audience who's listening to your interview.

"(HOST'S NAME), I'd like your listeners to know they can get 25% off my new book at my website if they mention your name!" Or, "If you buy today and mention you heard me on your show, I'll give you a two for one deal. Buy one of my books and I'll give you a second book absolutely free. Oh, plus free shipping!"

Or, something similar! Come up with your own "special offer" and rehearse it. Be prepared to offer it at the end of the show or just before a sponsor/commercial break if permitted. Make it known and repeat it throughout the show, especially at the end. You can give out special code numbers that give listeners a discount on your products or a specific product when they go through your shopping cart if that's doable. For example, create different coupon codes per giveaway per show. When people enter in those codes (or coupons) in the shopping cart, you know where that order came from. Make the coupon codes easy to spell and easy to remember.

INTERVIEW **TIP** #9

Always slip your website address into the interview conversation ...

It goes without saying, always be prepared to slip in your website address(s) during your interview. "At MyWebsite.com, I mention xyz123 and what you're talking about ..." Or, "I have more information about that at my website, MyWebsite.com ..." Or, "You can listen to, read more and watch videos on this topic at my website, MyWebsite.com."

You'd be surprised how many authors are interviewed today on big TV and radio stations who do not have, promote or slip in their website address into the interview conversation. How do they expect to bring more attention to what they have to offer? When you're being interviewed, you only have a minuscule amount of time to get your message out and all the information you really want to share.

In reality, that means, in that window of time, you need to cover everything you want to share. So, what do you do? Give out your website, where interested listeners can learn more about who you are, your products, articles, what more you have to say, but didn't get a chance to finish, etc.

INTERVIEW TIP #10

Practice with others who will ask you questions and you answer back ...

This is very helpful when you're just starting out. Have your list of questions written down and printed out, so a friend, family member, business associate, etc., can interview you. Practice giving your answers. Keep them short, yet detailed. Ask for constructive feedback from the person who interviewed you. How did you sound? Do you need to come up with more material for a specific question? Do you need to shorten the response time for a specific question? Record your interview so you can listen to it for constructive "suggestions and corrections" on how you answer, how long your answers are, etc. Practice makes perfect, so, keep practicing to continually improve and master your performance.

BONUS NOTES, IDEAS & MATERIAL

It's been mentioned before, but remember to send a "Thank you!" note to the person who interviewed you. Perhaps, they chose to interview you among many others. Show them your appreciation for helping to bring attention to your business and/or topic of expertise. And, if you made money from being interviewed (i.e., sales from the radio show), don't necessarily tell them you made any sales, but do thank them for having you on their show! At a minimum, you owe your appreciation!

Dear HOST NAME,

I just wanted to write and say thank you for having me on your show. I had a great time! I hope your audience enjoyed it, and that you too, were pleased with the interview session!

Please, think of me the next time you need another guest to help cover the subject we covered in the interview, or if you think of another topic you feel I would also be an interview candidate for ... I'm all yours! Just let me know.

Oh, by the way, I'm posting a link inside my Media Room (at my website) to your website about our interview. I hope it leads to a few more eyes and ears (traffic) for you and your show, too!

Again, thank you very much!

Your Name
(000) 000-0000 CELL/TEXT
YourWebsite.com

- I mentioned it earlier in the book that *"thank you" should be noted* in the form of a card by U.S. mail to them following a quick note via eMail. You might also leave a message via voice mail saying the same thing. It does wonders, be no one else does that! Nobody mails anything any more; especially to say *"Thank You!"*

- One way you'll stand out is by taking the time to say, *"Thank you!"* That always makes a host feel great and it might even get you back on the show, again. A good thing! *"Yes, the last time you were on the show we talked about ... What's new and exciting in the field of (your topic) ....?"*, and, your response? *"A lot! Let me tell you what's hot ... "*

- Ask the host, co-host or even the producer if you can get a quick testimonial from them (on the phone or via eMail you send them to reply to) about you being a guest on their show. Did they enjoy you being on their show? Did their audience enjoy you? Did the producer like working with you? Where you a great guest?

The answers to these questions, in the form of a testimonial on your site or inside your press kit, will help you secure your next interview in a flash! Why? Because if one show host likes you, chances are, the next one will too! Piggy-back one successful interview after the other, until you have a pile of interviews stacked up and everyone wants to interview you! NOTE: If you have a **TVGuest.com** directory profile listing, you can send them to your profile and submit a glowing REVIEW about your appearance.

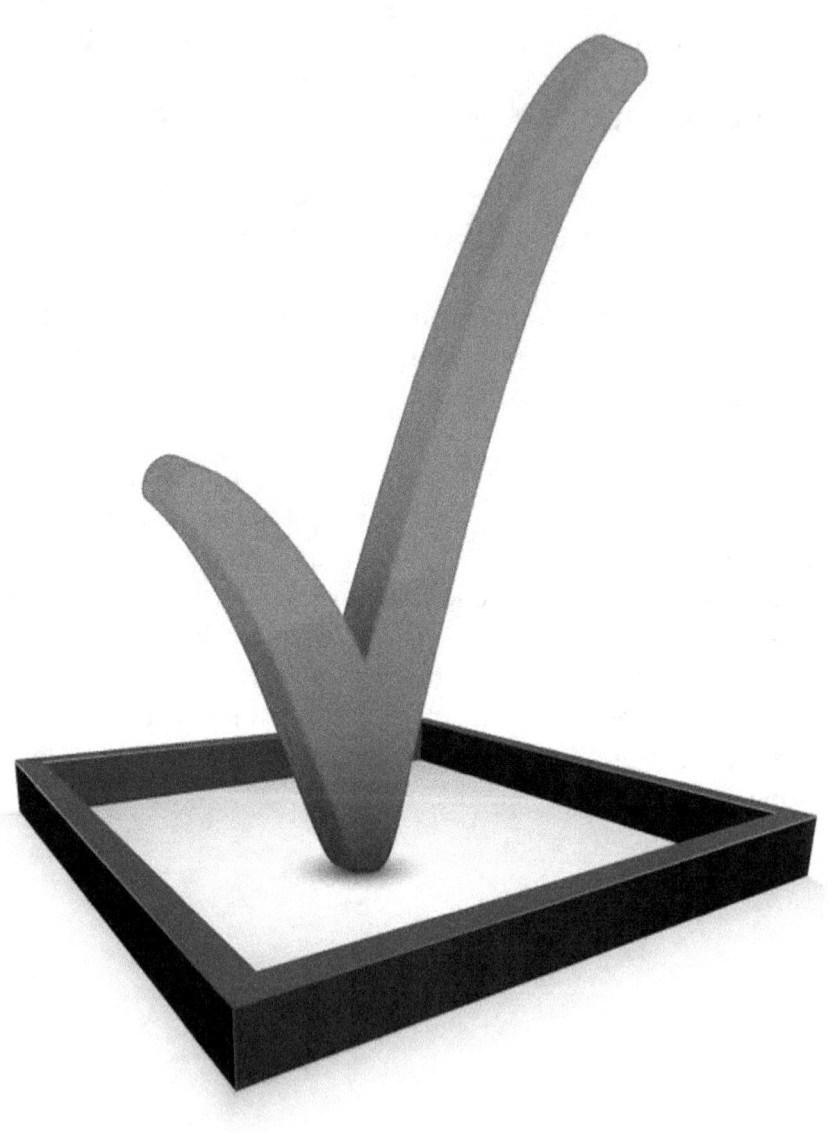

PART 7

My Personal TV/Radio
Interview Checklist

TVGuest.com

If one of your goals as an expert in your field of expertise is to showcase a book, product, service, website, to build your brand or reputation, ... getting interviews is a fast and free public relations strategy. With more than 5,000+ high-level radio talk shows, 50,000+ online talk shows, and 1,000+ TV news and talk shows, ... interviews have proven to reach enormous audiences. Getting started, you need to identify your niche, find what media your customers in your niche consume, and get to know who the radio, TV, and podcast hosts are, which is why it's important to use my checklist to help.

1.0 PREPARE FOR THE PERFECT INTERVIEW

1.1 _____ Since most radio interviews are conducted by telephone or online via video, **choose a quiet place in your home/office where you can speak freely and without interruptions.** Lock the door if necessary and let others know that you are behind closed doors for an important call. Sit in your car or in your garage if needed. You get the idea.

1.2 _____ **Prepare interview questions, stories and talking points** to cover the period of time that you expect to be interviewed. Interviews typically last 30-60-90 minutes.

1.3 _____ **Be prepared to answer any and all questions** regarding your topic and know it well. Your responses should be concise yet fully informational because you only have a very short period of time to make your case.

1.4 _____ If you want, **obtain a toll-free number unless your website is the best way to contact you.** People often remember names versus numbers so if you get a toll-free number, get one that spells something such as your name, your product or service in the number, for example, 1-888-GETMYBOOK. Go to

TollFreeNumbers.com or search 800#'s online to check it out.

1.5. ____ Is your website domain name easy to say, spell, remember? If you don't have a website yet, at least secure a domain name before your competition gets the same idea.

1.6. ____ If you're being interviewed on a large radio or TV station, direct listeners and viewers to a website that first captures their eMail addresses. Then have an opt-in form ready to redirect them to where your book (or product) is sold. Capture the customers' names/eMail addresses and then push for a sale! Make a special offer such as a discount for buying more than one of your books. Instruct them to "Go to MyDomain.com to claim your FREE _____ when you buy my book at any retail store. Make sure you're on my list to qualify. If you don't enter to win, you won't qualify for the FREE gift."

1.7. ____ Aim to be cordial, entertaining, informative, and respectful. Make sure that what you have to say is newsworthy and of genuine interest to your target market and don't be tempted to wander off topic.

2.0 HOW TO GET A RADIO INTERVIEW

2.1 ____ Go to Radio-Locator.com to look up radio stations throughout the USA. This is helpful when looking for local radio stations as well. Ideally, it's best if you can secure a radio interview at the station. Be sure that you get pictures with them before you leave so you can post them on your website or press room.

2.2 ____ You can search online for interview opportunities by using the keywords "be a radio guest" via Google. Search for online radio shows that cater to your business or topic. Also, go to BlogTalkRadio.com and other online radio station websites to locate specific stations that cater to your needs. I can recommend LATalkRadio.com. Their radio hosts are always looking for great guests. The number of opportunities you have for getting interviewed are virtually endless!

2.3 _____ **Learn the producer's name and/or others that work at the station or company** you're trying to get an interview with. Look for links on their websites that might read, "Become A Guest" or similar. You could also call the station and ask, "Do you interview guest experts on your show?" Most will respond with a YES answer. Convincing them that you are a viable guest expert for theirs shows is the fun part. This is your chance to show your creativity and enthusiasm. Here are a more tips.

2.4 _____ **If you can't give the station representative an overview of what you'd like to talk about, send a preview of the topic you wish to be interviewed for such as a new book, company, service, product, etc.** This information could also be posted on your website or in your press room. A page on your website could be dedicated to convincing radio station hosts and producers to book you for interviews. It has all the information they need in one place to make a quick decision. What you want to hear from them is, "Wow, this looks impressive. Yes, let's schedule a date/time to bring you into the station. Do you have your calendar handy?"

2.5 _____ **Provide the potential interview host/producer with endorsements for your book** from customers, clients, celebrities, experts, industry gurus, and anyone who is a fan of your work.

2.6 _____ **Provide endorsements from other talk show hosts** that have interviewed you in the past and/or links to their websites (and yours) where this information is posted. The more you have to offer, the more in demand you become. Start small, such as local stations, and continually build your reputation!

2.7 _____ **Depending on the method you use to send your material, include press releases**, copies of your recent eZine/newsletter, flyer, postcard, one-sheet, articles published online/offline showcasing your profession and accomplishments. Ideally, this should be on a one-pager on your website where you can refer interviewers to a specific link having all the information they require.

2.8 _____ **Don't forget to follow up 2-3 days after you send in your proposal for an interview and then follow up again if you don't get a response back within 10 days.** Follow up with a phone call and/or eMail (or both) if you must leave a message. Another way to get their attention is to send a postcard with your book cover (for example) as a reminder that you are still interested in their station and speaking to their audience of listeners.

2.9 _____ **If you can't get in touch with the producer or show host, talk to and/or befriend a representative of the station.** Send a gift (for me it's my world famous chocolate chip cookies), an autographed copy of your book, sample products you produce, etc. If you don't get the kind of response you're looking for immediately, don't give up. Keep the station updated on what's happening in your world, notifications of other interviews, a new product, etc.

3.0 WHAT TO DO BEFORE THE INTERVIEW

3.1 _____ **Listen to previously recorded/archived shows to get a feel for how a particular host interacts with guests.**

Also, pick up on talking points other guests or listeners or callers have made. You can bring them up in your interview if appropriate to make a stronger impact on the host and their audience. "I recall one of your previous guests talked about _____. That's an interesting point because _____. " Become the guest expert that get's invited back again and again!

3.2. _____ **Be sure that the station you are targeting has the best numbers to contact you and vice versa.** Use caller I.D. to watch for their calls. Typically, a producer or staff member will contact you and connect you with the host of the show. Get that person's name and be sure that you thank (name) for patching you through.

3.3. _____ **What time of the day is the radio show? How long is the show?** Be aware of varying time zones when soliciting numerous stations.

3.4. _____ **How long will your interview be? Practice interviewing for period of time until you feel confident about what you'll say.** Some interviews might be 15 minutes, 30 minutes or even longer. Will you be prepared to speak for two hours? When participating in a radio interview, it's live, obviously, and it's your big chance to make yourself known. Never go unprepared.

3.5. _____ **Get the host's direct eMail address at the station so you let the person know how much you are looking forward to the interview.** Include any press material or samples of your work if possible. You'll want to send them a thank you note after the interview as well.

3.6. _____ **Research the host on the radio station's website.** The more you know about your host for the show, the more comfortable you'll be speaking to him/her. Be aware of current events in their area/town/state if needed to present a power-packed, informative interview.

3.7 _____ **Does the host accept call-ins?** This would be very good to know in advance so you're not caught off guard. You might want to prepare yourself with sample scenarios, case studies, and more to respond to questions beyond what the host is prepared to ask you about.

3.8 _____ **Ask the producer what information you can freely give to your fans such as your website,** toll free number or other number, eMail address, etc. Confirmation on the small things go a long way when it comes to building rapport with the gatekeeper of the show you're going to be a guest on.

3.9 _____ **Suggest to the host that you will give away something (i.e., product, book, audio program) to 1-3 lucky winners before, during, and/or at the end of the show.** Be sure to get the winner's full name, eMail address, mailing address and phone number. Then, personally autograph what you're sending and include a note that explains, "Congratulations on winning _____ on as announced on the _____ radio show last week." You can include a mini-catalog or one-sheet of your other products/services when you mail out the prizes. Include several business cards for distribution. This is a great opportunity to network.

3.10 _____ **Ask the radio host if you could provide the show with a pre-recorded mini-commercial to promote your upcoming interview.** You can record this on your computer, then save it to an MP3 and eMail it to the show as an attachment for their use. For example, you might record something like, "Hi, this is Bart Smith, author of LAWS OF THE BEDROOM. If you'd like to learn more about (topic), tune in to the (name radio show and station, date plus date and time). Join in on the conversation!" Ask the producer of the show if this is feasible. They might have the perfect script prepared for you.

3.11 ____ Does the TV or radio station have any relationships with bookstores or other entities suitable for your product? If you are promoting a new book, your local bookstores might be interested in a book signing at their locations knowing that you are scheduled for a TV or radio interview. Your interview could promote more business by driving more customers to their stores. Remember to video record and/or take photos of your book signing events for promotional purposes.

3.12 ____ Is there any topic that might be off limits (by you or the station) for your interview? Don't be caught unaware and say something you'll regret or that will ruin your chances of future interview gigs.

4.0 RECORDING INTERVIEWS

4.1 ____ If your interview is recorded, ask for a copy. Ask for permission to use it to promote your business online and offline. If your interview is recorded and the station is unwilling or unable (for any reason) to give you a copy, direct your audience to the station's website. If you obtain a recorded copy of the interview, post it on your website.

4.2 ____ Post all your recorded interviews in your press room afterwards so future hosts and producers can go to that page and listen to how you interview. Your interview could potentially inspire other stations to pick you up. If all else fails, recreate the interview using another interviewer utilizing the same questions and content discussed on the show. This is a great way to bring home the powerful message you delivered on the show that you can now use with full copyright privileges.

4.3 ____ Does the host of the show where you'll be interviewed blog? Consider asking them to blog about your upcoming interview. This will give you the chance to create a back link to your website and share valuable information with your readership. Be your own reporter. After the interview, discuss the outcome of the show on your blog. By having reciprocal links with the show, you both stand to gain in traffic and appeal. It's a powerful link activity.

5.0 MEDIA INTERVIEW TECHNIQUES

5.1 ____ Not all interviewers are experts on the topics they cover, which is why they rely on experts for facts and commentary. Depending on the media you choose to interview with, learn the names of the producer, host, former guests, previous show titles, staff members and more. No two interviews will ever be the same so your goal in an interview is to get your message across.

5.2 ____ Know the radio station call letters (i.e., KFIZ, KQV, WDAY, KWAM, WOC, WBBZ, etc.) as needed.

5.3 ____ Know the frequency of the stations (i.e., Newstalk 1290, 1065 AM, 95.5 FM, etc.).

5.4 ____ Know contact numbers such as main office, direct or emergency contact telephone number in case you get bumped off of a call. This happened to me once. I was on an interview with a radio station and I was accidentally dropped. Luckily, I had the station's phone number handy and called back immediately. I didn't want to rely on them to call me back. As there were several other guest experts on the call, I took matters into my own hands and was immediately reconnected within a couple of minutes.

5.5 _____ Who is hosting the show and do they have any co-hosts? Be certain that you can pronounce everyone's name properly. If you're uncertain, ask and don't wing it. Be certain you have the correct spelling for written communications. You might write the names on piece of paper at a glance to ensure that you don't make any mistakes. This goes for any other information you might need to refer to. Consider creating a one-sheet with everything you need to know and it's ready at your fingertips.

5.6 _____ While conducting a radio interview, feel free to take notes about a topic/question you want to respond to. When you and your host have finished with your talking points, look at your notes for any last detail you wanted to bring up. Make every effort to keep the interview smooth and free-flowing to avoid sounding confused or unorganized.

5.7 _____ PREPARE for the interview days in advance of the interview. This is a case where practice makes perfect. Research the station and demographics of the show. Know who their listeners are such as gender, age group, etc. and tailor your interview toward that audience; good for you and good for the show.

5.8 _____ Secure the date of the interview and put in on your online/offline calendars and then schedule time to practice and prepare for your interview.

6.0 WHAT TO SEND PRIOR TO THE INTERVIEW

6.1 _____ After you ask which method of communication the host and/or producer prefers such as telephone, eMail and/or regular postal mail prior to the interview taking place, send a letter to confirm that you know the time, the place, and the subject matter of the interview and how much you're looking forward to it. Include benefits for their listening audience and propose a plan to promote your interview on their show.

6.2 ____ Provide a biography including your accomplishments. Send a short biography that the host can read on the air and a more detailed one so the host can learn more about you. Even though the show can access this information on your site, send either an electronic copy or a hard copy so you know they have it.

6.3 ____ Include your website and specific page links to where you archive information for your press room and/or media purposes. Provide specific page links to your biography, samplings of previous interviews, press releases, etc. Make it easy to find, for example, http://YourSite.com/press room or /press kit ... etc.

6.4 ____ Send an eMail the day before the interview to acknowledge that you are enthusiastically anticipating the opportunity to interview the show. This can reassure them that you're on top of things and you haven't forgotten about the interview that was booked possibly a month ago. Include a link to your website where you are currently promoting the upcoming interview and the respective RV/radio station. If you record this information on your website, the station might want to listen in.

6.5 ____ Send multiple (autographed) copies of your book, not just one. Ask if they'd like a couple to be sent. The wholesale cost of your book multiplied by 2-5 books is nothing compared to the value of exposure and notoriety you're going to get when you get interviewed on their show. Most hosts will read them or either skip through them before, or even during the show! Also, don't expect the host not to know too much about your book. Don't make them look badly in front of their listeners, but help them to do their job well!

6.6 ____ Send 10-20 suggested questions to the host with suggested answers that you'd like to be asked. Some hosts will ask the questions you provide them verbatim. Others will creatively tweak your questions or come up with their own. Don't be shocked or offended, but be prepared if they don't ask any of your questions and come up with their own. The answers help the host craft even more questions or topics for discussion.

6.7 ____ Send the host/producer one-sheet with your full name, contact information and a brief description of your book/product/service and how the audience can obtain what you offer. I suggest you print the 8 ½ x 11 sheet using 16 font size for easy reading so the host can refer to it while speaking live.

6.8 ____ Have the answers to questions and page numbers (if referencing your new book). Don't be caught off guard not knowing your topic or how to answer a question. If possible, ask for a set of questions that the host will be asking so you can prepare in advance of the interview so it goes smoothly.

6.9 ____ If you are invited to the studio or station where the interview will be conducted, take extra copies of your book or samples of your product. Dress appropriately for the occasion and be prepared to ask for photographs with the host, producer and staff. If your interview is scheduled for live television, ask for tips on what to wear and what colors work best for TV viewers. Take pictures with your cell phone of the name of the studio inside/outside of the building for display on your website. If you don't get a recording of the show, you will at least have photos to share with your audience!

6.10 ____ Mention the station's call letters during the show whenever you get the chance. It helps the host remind listeners of the show's brand. You might say, "Thank you, (Host Name), for having me on your show here on NewsTalk 1290." Mention the host by name throughout the interview. It's all about exposure and branding and reciprocal promotions help you both particularly when you have such a broad reach of listeners unique to radio's listening audience.

6.11 ____ If your book is not ready for release, especially by the time of your interview, direct everyone to a name squeeze page where you collect their names and eMail addresses. Start building your list before the book is available. Picture offering 1-10 winners a chance to win a FREE copy of your book or product! The cost for shipping a few FREE books/products pales to 500 people who sign up to buy having viewed or heard you on a TV/radio station interview.

7.0 PLUGGING YOUR OWN BOOK, PRODUCT, SERVICE or WEBSITE

If you sense that the host is not promoting your book/product enough, then take advantage of the opportunity to plug it yourself, professionally, but with gusto. How often?

a) ____ Once in the BEGINNING

b) ____ Once in the MIDDLE

c) ____ Several times THROUGHOUT (especially if it's a 45+ minute interview)

d) ____ Once at the END

8.0 WHAT TO DO AFTER THE INTERVIEW

8.1 _____ Be prepared to send post cards designed with your book cover on one side and an area on the other side to write a thank you message to everyone that helped you through the interview process. This goes for any product or service you may be promoting.

8.2 _____ If you haven't already done this, be sure to contact the station to ask if you can eMail or fax one sheet containing all your contact information related to how listeners can reach you and/or buy your book/product/service. Since the receptionist is usually the only person a viewer or listener can reach, it's best to leave the information with the receptionist first and then ask to pass it along to other staff who might interact with listeners who call in. This one sheet should contain your full name, company name, telephone number, website, eMail address, book title (if selling a book) or product/service details. A one page website works for this.

8.3 _____ If you had a good experience at the radio/TV station, recommend others to contact them to inquire about interviewing opportunities. Suggest they use your name as a referral. "My friend/associate was just interviewed by you, and I was wondering how I might get interviewed. My expertise is on _____." When sending your thank you letter, you could include names and contact information for those that you recommend. This is another way to network with people.

8.4 _____ Within the following 24-48 hours, ask for a testimonial while the information is fresh. Also as the host or producer for approval to post any testimonial or endorsement on your website or use it in any marketing promotion: "(Your Name) was a superb guest on my show, (ENTER TITLE). I would definitely interview them again and I recommend others do the

THAT'S A WRAP

My TV/Radio Interview Tactics & Checklists
Summary & Words Of Encouragement

WOW, YOU MADE IT! What did you learn? Hopefully, you picked up a 100+ great tips and strategies to tune up your efforts in going after interviews. Now, go get 100+ interviews and start promoting yourself like a ROCK STAR. After your first 10-20 interviews, you'll be ready for larger audiences. Pretty soon, you'll be ready for TV, and, well, who knows what's next?

With literally 1,000's of potential shows you could be on, don't be picky. Just start! Try to do 1-3 interviews per week. You don't have to maintain that schedule, but when you're getting started, it's best to do at least one a week. Try getting to the point where you can do 3-5 per week. Schedule 2 during the same day. Either way, the more you do, the more they'll benefit you.

Before you know it, show hosts will be reaching out to you. This says something about YOU getting out there and getting scene and heard. When THIS snowball starts to happen, look out, because it's only a matter of time before your audiences really starts to expand and you're asked to be on bigger and bigger shows. Revisit what you've learned about interview preparation so that from your own experience those skills are soon at the level of success you hope to achieve.

Hey, having said all that, I wish you the very best in all of your interview pursuits!

Bart Smith, Founder
BartSmith.com
ReallyFastBooks.com
ReallyCheapNames.com
TVGuest.com

Get A Profile Listing On TVGuest.com & Get More Interviews

NOTES NOTES NOTES

After reading **MY TV/RADIO INTERVIEW TACTICS & CHECKLISTS!**, what stood out for you? What kind of actionable items regarding interviews do you need to act on? Take a few moments to reflect and jot down a few notes that could help you and then make it happen!

ABOUT THE AUTHOR

BART SMITH

Like many authors, BART SMITH aspires to share his books and lessons learned. Having written 30+ books, you know he's busy giving lots of interviews. He needs to be ready! So, how does he prepare? He refers to the book he wrote on how to get interviewed! As the founder of **TVGuest.com**, he also knew it would be helpful if his clients had a book to consult with before getting interviewed!

If you enjoy listening to audiobooks, Bart has recorded this book in audio format for you to listen to as well, including this book. Listen to them for free at *BartSmith.com/audio*.

One of BART'S PASSIONS (and business pursuits) is baking the world's best chocolate chip cookies since 1988. Really, check it out at **BartsCookies.com** ...

BART'S BOOKS, TRAINING WEBSITE & MORE

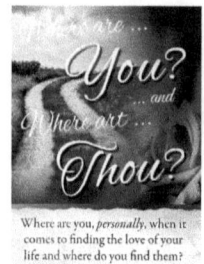
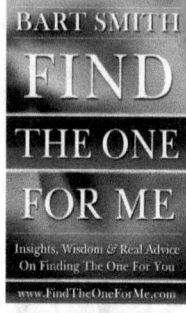

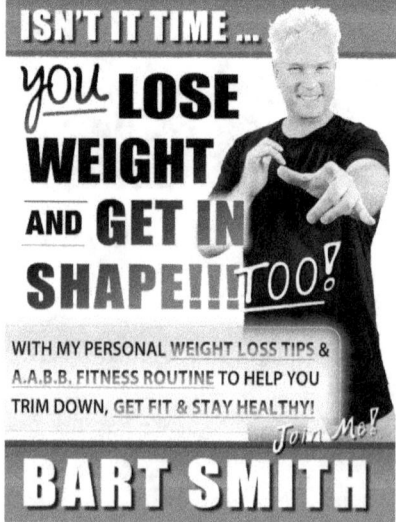

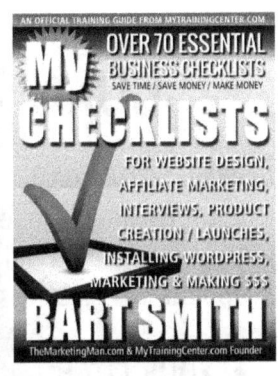

COACHING & CONSULTING

Being a TV guest isn't something we do every day, so it's vital you consider some amount of coaching and consulting by a trained professional. Consider these areas to ensure your TV guest appearance is an Oscar award-winning success:

- **YOUR PITCH** – If you'd like us to find TV shows for you, let's review your pitch so we can best represent you to the different TV stations we're aligned with. What's more, **do you have a book?** Talk to us about our "really fast" book publishing services to help you get on TV with a book as an author!

- **INTERVIEW QUESTIONS** – If you don't have interview questions ready, we'll help you create them and place them on your website. These are suggested questions you want the TV host to ask you.

- **WEBSITE / LEAD GENERATION / SALES SYS. AUDIT** – How is your website? Do you have one? Is it ready to receive the kind of high-profile exposure and potential lead / sales you could get?

- **PRE-TV SHOW PREPARATIONS** – This could include a variety of things that range anywhere from on-camera presence/practice, interview training/practice answering questions, practicing call-to-action statements, arranging transportation to/from the TV show, checklists for what to bring/do/say before/during/after your TV guest appearance and much, much more.

- **POST-TV SHOW REVIEW** – This can be a meeting in-person or over the telephone, Web/Zoom/Skype, etc., where we discuss how you performed. We'll review what you did well and offer any areas for improvement if needed. For more information about these services, contact us online!

TVGuest.com/coaching

CLASSES & ONLINE E-COURSE

LIVE IN-PERSON CLASSES (3 HRS)

If you're ever in the Los Angeles area, you might want to attend one of Bart's live in-person training classes where he share how to become a TV guest on TV shows.

TOPICS COVERED INCLUDE:

- How to become a TV guest on TV shows ...

- How to prepare to be a great TV guest ...

- What to do before/during/after your TV guest appearance on TV shows ...

- How to get asked back to other TV shows ... *and much more!*

For more information about our classes, dates/times/locations, and how to register for our next one, visit the link below!

ONLINE E-COURSE (3 HRS)

If you can't make it to one of our live in-person classes, we've **recorded the LIVE IN-PERSON CLASS for your convenience via online viewing/learning.** You can enroll in the online course 24/7/365. We cover the same material as the class, with a few perks for online students because we can do things online that we can't offline. So, check it out by visiting the link below.

WE KNOW YOU'LL LOVE THIS INSPIRING COURSE!

www.TVGuest.com/events

VIDEO RECORDING SERVICES

Do you have video of yourself? Depending on the video you do or don't have, we highly recommend you film yourself in an interview setting either talking about your book, company, products and/or services, but in a way that serves the TV host and his/her audience.

Remember, never sell directly on TV when you're a TV guest. Save that for QVC! Instead, tell stories, answer questions with sound-bite answers, and at the end, you'll get a window of time to give your contact information if anyone's interested in learning more about you.

How do you know what you look like on camera or how you'll do when interviewed? How does a prospective TV show person know how you look or interview on camera? Let's find out! Schedule time with us to film you in a mock interview setting for use on your website as well for use on your TVGuest.com profile listing.

We'll help you prepare, rehearse and film you answering interview questions on-camera as if it was a real TV show appearance. Not only is this a good warm up for the real thing, you also get a video interview clip that you can use on your website and social media to promote you for other types of interviews. Interested in this service? Go to:

TVGuest.com/services

LEADS FOR "TV GUEST SPOTS"

WHO'S ASKING: In the TV show world, there are TV show personnel that don't always have time to look over your website to find the perfect TV guest and would rather ask us directly who we know and can recommend as the best person for their TV show. Well, when we get contacted by people representing TV shows like this, we call these **"TV GUEST SPOT" LEADS!** and we get dozens per DAY!

HOW IT WORKS: When we get a "TV GUEST SPOT" LEAD we listen to their TV guest requirements and let them know, *"Yes, we have a few candidates for you to choose from whom we think would be the perfect TV guest to fill your TV GUEST SPOT."* Once we know what type of TV guest they need, we'll reach out immediately to our TV GUEST SPOT LEADS list for availability and interest in their TV guest spot. For the TVGuest.com member who accepts this lead, we'll share the name of the person, TV show and contact information so they can go over the particulars of getting on their TV show.

FIRST COME, FIRST SERVE: TV GUEST SPOT LEADS come and go quickly! Everyone wants these leads because they're HOT! The TVGuest.com member who jumps at the opportunity and scores the acceptance of the TV show is the winner of that TV GUEST SPOT LEAD. Don't worry, we get TV GUEST SPOT LEADS daily if you missed one.

FEES FOR THIS SERVICE: There are two separate admin fees to participate in this pool of TV GUEST SPOT LEADS. There's an annual fee to be on the TV GUEST SPOT LEAD list and a fee every time the TVGuest.com member actually accepts a TV show spot.

WHY BE ON THIS LIST? If you want to get on TV faster, take advantage of these HOT leads that come into our office daily! Why wait for someone to contact you, when we could recommend you today and have you on a TV show tomorrow? For more info, go to:

TVGuest.com/leads

TVGUEST.COM

DIRECTORY "PROFILE LISTING"

WHAT IS IT? Directory profile listings on TVGuest.com quickly and publicly showcases your profile as an expert, someone who's written a book or experienced something TV show hosts want to feature on their show for the benefit of their audience members.

WHY HAVE A PROFILE LISTING ON TVGUEST.COM? While most websites get lost in space like grains of sand on the beach, TVGuest.com members stand out to everyone in the TV world who's looking to find guests for their TV shows. Sure, they could go to other websites that help reporters, but many are already stopping by TVGuest.com first to find qualified candidates and fast! Exactly!

WHAT DO YOU GET WITH YOUR TVGUEST.COM LISTING? While there are different membership levels you can subscribe to, in general, every member gets to publicly display all of the following to help win over the minds of potential TV show personnel decision-makers looking to book TV guests for their TV shows. It displays:

★ Name / Title / Profession
★ Contact Info (Phone# / eMail)
★ Bio / About / Description
★ Upload Audio & Video
★ Upload Articles & Photos
★ Post Events & MORE!

SELF-MANAGED TVGUEST.COM PROFILE LISTINGS: That's right! You get to create, login and maintain your own profile listing yourself. This is perfect when you want to add more content to your profile such as new videos, photos and articles, update your contact info, etc.

TVGUEST.COM PROFILE LISTING COST: While we are always running specials, if you consider as an investment in you making more money and getting more exposure via TV, write this off as a tax-deductible advertising expense and get listed today!

TVGuest.com/listing

Your Name

TV/Radio Guest Prospect
www.YourWebsite.com
Your Town, ST 00000

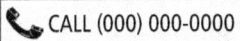

📞 CALL (000) 000-0000

Contact This Guest   **Review This Guest**

💬 MAKE A CONNECTION! Your Name is currently available to chat. **Contact This TV Guest!**

Overview   Interview Categories (3)   Articles (5)   Photo Albums (3)   Videos (7)

Contact Information:

Website	http://YourWebsite.com
Social Profiles	🇫 🇹 in 📺 8+ 🔊 📷 Ⓦ
Telephone	000-000-0000
One-Sheet	View My Curriculum / Brochure
Travels From	Your Town, State
Availability	🎬 In-Studio
	🖥 Online via Skype
	🎵 Telephone Interview
	📄 Q&A Article Format
	✈ Nationwide by Arrangement
	⏱ Last-Minute
Credentials	Enter your credentials, awards, recognition statements, accomplishments, etc., in your field of experience or experience to impress potential TV show personnel looking for the right kind of guest.
Interview Questions	http://YourWebsite.com/interview-questions

GET YOUR LISTING TODAY!

Interview Show/Ideas:

ENTER SHOW IDEA/TITLE HERE (i.e., PROBLEM) THAT PROVOKES CURIOSITY & IS VERY NICHE FOCUSED IN RELATION TO YOUR EXPERTISE/EXPERIENCE/TRAINING

Write 1-2 paragraphs that describe the problem out in the world and perhaps what's not being done about it. This problem/topic is what you want to be interviewed on because you're the expert that can solve this problem, shed light on it, explain it better, set the record straight, etc.

· List how people are suffering from this problem ...
· What's common among people with this problem ...

TVGuest.com

"PROFILE LISTING" CATEGORIES

These categories represent niche subjects TV and radio shows need guests for. Peruse these category titles. Could you speak effectively on any one (or more) of these topics? Within each category, there are 5-10 sub-categories worth of topics that show hosts also need guests for. What does that mean? It means 1,000's of experts are needed daily, weekly, monthly to speak with confidence on 1,000+ topics! WOW!

ADD & ADHD
Abuse
Accountability
Achievement
Addiction / Recovery
Adoption / Fostering
Adult Entertainment
Adventurers
Advertising
African-American
Aging / Anti-Aging
Alcoholism
American History
American Legends
Anger Management
Animals
Archaeology
Art Performances
Arts & Pop Culture
Athletics / Sports
Attitude
Author
Autism
Awareness & Prevention
Body Language
Branding
Bullying
Business
Business Building
Business Entrepreneurship
Business Growth
Business Trends
Business of Healthcare
Cancer
Cancer Awareness

Career
Celebrity
Celebrity Chefs
Celebrity Speakers
Change
Character Portrayals
China
Christian
Chronic Diseases
Cirque / Acrobats
Coaching
College/University
Comedy
Communication
Communities
Community Relations
Competition
Conflict Resolution
Construction / Building
Consulting
Consumer Trends
Corporate Culture
Corporate Responsibility
Corporate Social Responsibility
Creativity
Crisis
Cultural
Cultural Diversity
Customer Service
Dental Health / Tooth Care
Difficult People
Disability Issues
Disaster Recovery
Domestic Violence
Drug Abuse

Eating Disorders
Ecommerce / Online Sales
Economy
Education
Elementary Education
Emotional Balance
Employees / Workforce
Empowerment
Energy (Oil, Gas, etc.)
Entertainment
Entrepreneurship
Environmental
Environmental Policy
Ethics & Values
Etiquette
Exercise / Fitness
Facilitator
Family
Finance & Insurance
Financial Freedom
Food
Franchising
Freedom
Fundraising
Futurists
Gender Issues
Generation Issues
Global Business
Global Issues
Goal Setting
Government/Politics
Green Issues / Living
Grief
HIV, Aids & STD

Happiness
Health
Health & Beauty
Health & Nutrition
Healthcare Experts
Healthy Lifestyle
History
Home & Garden
Home Health / Care Giving
Homeland Security
Human / Sex Trafficking
Human Resources
Humor
Identity Theft & Safety
Image / Self Esteem
Innovation & Creativity
Inspiration
International Affairs
Internet / World Wide Web
Internet Marketing
Investing / Financial Issues
Judicial System
Language
Law
Law of Attraction
Leadership
Learning Disorders
Life After Work
Life At Work
Life Balance
Lifestyle
Listening Skills
Magic / Illusion
Management
Marketing
Master of Ceremonies
Media
Medical
Men
Mental Health
Mentalists & Hypnotists
Metaphysics
Midlife Transitions
Military
Military / Veterans
Mind / Body Medicine
Money Mindset

Motivation
NLP
Negotiation
Networking
News & Current Events
Nutrition
Olympic Athletes
Organizational Skills
Overcoming Adversity
Parenting & Children
Patriotism
Peak Performance
Performance Improvement
Personal / Life Coaching
Personal Development
Personal Safety
Personality Testing
Pets
Photography
Political
Political Humor
Presentation Skills
Productivity
Profitability
Prosperity
Psychology
Publicity / Public Relations
Real Estate
Reality TV Stars
Recruitment & Retention
Relationships
Religion
Restaurant Industry
Retail
Retirement / Aging
Revues & Variety Shows
Risk Management
Safety
Sales
Science & Engineering
Security
Self Empowerment
Self Help
Self-Publishing
Sex & Sensuality
Sex Education
Sexual Abuse

Small Business
Social Causes
Social Media
Social Services
Spirituality
Sports
Spouse Programs
Strategic Planning
Stress & Anxiety
Success
Succession Planning
Suicide Awareness
Sustainability
TED Conference
TEDX Conference
Tax Planning
Team Building
Technology
Teens
Time Management
Top News
Travel/Tourism
Vaccines
Videography
Vision / Eyesight
Vision / Purpose
Volunteerism
Web Design
Weight Loss
Wellness
Women
Women In Business
Women In Society
Work/Life Balance
Workplace Safety
Writing
Youth Issues

GET YOUR
LISTING
TODAY!

ON
TVGuest.com

"PROFILE LISTING" CONTENT

What do you get to advertise/showcase publicly in front of hundreds, if not thousands, of potential TV (and other) show hosts, directors, producers, agents, publicists, etc. all looking for expert guests to be on their shows? With your **TVGuest.com directory profile listing**, you get to add all of the following to your profile listing. For example, you can showcase:

☑ YOUR **FULL NAME**

☑ YOUR **COMPANY NAME**

☑ YOUR **PHONE NUMBER**

☑ YOUR **CITY/STATE** (LOCATION)

☑ YOUR **WEBSITE**

☑ YOUR **PHOTO** (PROFESSIONAL HEAD SHOT)

☑ YOUR **SOCIAL MEDIA ACCOUNTS** (VIA LINKS)

☑ YOUR **MEDIA ROOM** (VIA LINK)

☑ YOUR **INTERVIEW QUESTIONS** (VIA LINK)

☑ YOUR **AVAILABILITY** (IN-STUDIO, VIA PHONE, ETC.)

☑ YOUR **CREDENTIALS** (EXPERT BIO, DEGREES, ETC.)

☑ INTERVIEW **TOPICS/IDEAS** (ONE OR MORE)

☑ INTERVIEW **DESCRIPTIONS** (ONE OR MORE)

☑ **ARTICLES** (ABOUT YOUR INTERVIEW TOPICS)

☑ **PHOTOS** (ABOUT YOUR INTERVIEW TOPICS)

☑ **VIDEOS** (ABOUT YOUR INTERVIEW TOPICS)

☑ **EVENTS** (POST UPCOMING INTERVIEW DATES)

GET YOUR LISTING TODAY!

TVGUEST.COM

Pretty much everything you can add to your profile is interview-related, interview-focused, and rich with (your) contact information so TV and other show hosts know how to contact you immediately and without a middle-man (charging you an arm and a leg) to possibly book you for their next show!

"PROFILE LISTING" USES

Now that you know what a **TVGuest.com directory profile listing** looks like, the categories you can align yourself with, in addition to the content you can publicly display to help attract potential hosts to book you for their upcoming shows, the next question is, WHAT CAN YOU DO WITH your TVRG directory profile listing? Well, here are all the ways you can use your TVGuest.com directory profile listing:

☑ USE IT TO **PITCH ANY SHOW (YOURSELF)** – It's easy to pitch practically any type of show to interview for if you have all your interview-related/focused information in one place -- easy to find, easy to read/follow and easy to contact you! Why wouldn't you get booked *in a flash* for their next show?

☑ ALLOW TVRG STAFF TO **PITCH SHOWS (ON YOUR BEHALF)** – If you choose to have TVRG find TV (and other) shows for you to be interviewed on, one of the ways you make our job easy is to have a well-populated, interview-focused directory profile listing ready to go! We'll use it to pitch TV show hosts about you. Hopefully, you have (content) they're looking for!

☑ USE IT AS **YOUR RESUME** – Looking to get a job from a potential client? Send them to your TVGuest directory listing. They can see all your expertise, view credentials, follow social media links, and much more.

☑ USE IT AS **YOUR WEBSITE** – You might like to use your TVGuest.com directory listing profile as your actual website. Why? Because it costs even more money to build and maintain a separate website, let alone have time to build it. Considering the complexity of maintaining a website, why bother? Just use your TVRG directory listing to showcase what you do, link to your social media accounts, attract interviews/clients, and much more!

GET YOUR **TVGR DIRECTORY PROFILE LISTING** TODAY ... GO TO **TVGUEST.COM**